& the Written Word

Hodder & Stoughton

A MEMBER OF THE HODDER HEADLINE GROUP

Just the Job! draws directly on the CLIPS careers information database developed and maintained by Lifetime Careers Wiltshire and used by almost every careers service in the UK. The database is revised annually using a rigorous update schedule and incorporates material collated through desk/telephone research and information provided by all the professional bodies, institutions and training bodies with responsibility for course accreditation and promotion of each career area.

ISBN 0 340 68778 9
First published 1997

Impression number   10 9 8 7 6 5 4 3 2 1
Year   2002 2001 2000 1999 1998 1997

Copyright © 1997 Lifetime Careers Wiltshire Ltd

All rights reserved. No part of this publication may be reproduced or transmitted in any form or by any means, electronic or mechanical, including photocopy, recording or any information storage and retrieval system, without permission in writing from the publisher or under licence from the Copyright Licensing Agency Ltd. Further details of such licences (for reprographic reproduction) may be obtained from the Copyright Licensing Agency Ltd, 90 Tottenham Court Road, London W1P 9HE.

Printed in Great Britain for Hodder & Stoughton Educational, the educational publishing division of Hodder Headline Plc, 338 Euston Road, London NW1 3BH, by Cox & Wyman Ltd, Reading, Berkshire.

CONTENTS

Introduction	7
Writing for a living	10
Writing books. Scriptwriting. Freelance journalism. Copywriting. Technical writing. Indexing. Other jobs involving writing.	
Journalism	14
Newspaper journalism. Magazines. News agencies. Radio and television. Researchers.	
Technical writing	23
Working in libraries & information services	27
Information officer	37
Information scientist	41
Archivist	45
Publishing	48
Book publishing. Periodical publishing. Careers related to publishing.	
Desktop publishing	57
DTP in printing. General DTP work.	
Press photographer	60
Work with languages	63
Interpreters and translators. Teaching. Jobs with scope for using languages.	
Translating & interpreting	71
Working in the media	75
Journalism. Radio and television. Design. Photography. Film and video. Publishing. Advertising.	
Broadcasting – production & presentation	79
Research assistant. Presenter.	

Advertising	**82**
Advertising agencies. Advertising media. Advertising and publicity departments. Advertising services.	
Public relations	**86**
Politics	**89**
Party headquarters staff. Parliamentary jobs. Civil Service and local government work. Journalism.	
For further information	**91**

JUST THE JOB!

The *Just the Job!* series ranges over the entire spectrum of occupations and is intended to generate job ideas and stretch horizons of interest and possibility, allowing you to explore families of jobs for which you might have appropriate ability and aptitude. Each *Just the Job!* book looks in detail at a popular area or type of work, covering:

- ways into work;
- essential qualifications;
- educational and training options;
- working conditions;
- progression routes;
- potential career portfolios.

The information given in *Just the Job!* books is detailed and carefully researched. Obvious bias is excluded to give an even-handed picture of the opportunities available, and course details and entry requirements are positively checked in an annual update cycle by a team of careers information specialists. The text is written in approachable, plain English, with a minimum of technical terms.

In Britain today, there is no longer the expectation of a career for life, but support has increased for life-long learning and the acquisition of skills which will help young and old to make sideways career moves – perhaps several times during a working life – as well as moving into work carrying higher levels of responsibility and reward. *Just the Job!* invites you to select an appropriate direction for your *own* career progression.

Educational and vocational qualifications

A level – Advanced level of the General Certificate of Education
AS level – Advanced Supplementary level of the General Certificate of Education (equivalent to half an A level)
BTEC – Business and Technology Education Council: awards qualifications such as BTEC First, BTEC National Certificate/Diploma, etc
GCSE – General Certificate of Secondary Education
GNVQ/GSVQs – General National Vocational Qualification/ General Scottish Vocational Qualification: awarded at Foundation, Intermediate and Advanced levels by BTEC, City & Guilds of London Institute, Royal Society of Arts and SCOTVEC
HND/C – BTEC Higher National Diploma/Certificate
International Baccalaureate – recognised by all UK universities as equivalent to a minimum of two A levels
NVQ/SVQs – National/Scottish Vocational Qualifications: awarded by the National Council for Vocational Qualifications and the Scottish Vocational Education Council
SCE – Scottish Certificate of Education, at **Standard** Grade (equate directly with GCSEs: grades 1–3 in SCEs at Standard Grade are equivalent to GCSE grades A–C) and **Higher** Grade (equate with the academic level attained after one year of a two-year A level course: three to five Higher Grades are broadly equivalent to two to four A levels at grades A–E)

Vocational work-based credits	NVQ/SVQ level 1	NVQ/SVQ level 2	NVQ/SVQ level 3	NVQ/SVQ level 4
Vocational qualifications: *a mix of theory and practice*	Foundation GNVQ/ GSVQ; BTEC First	Intermediate GNVQ/GSVQ	Advanced GNVQ/GSVQ; BTEC National Diploma/Certificate	BTEC Higher National Diploma/ Certificate
Educational qualifications	GCSE/SCE Standard Grade pass grades	GCSE grades A–C; SCE Standard Grade levels 1–3	Two A levels; four Scottish Highers; Baccalaureate	University degree

INTRODUCTION

This book focuses on careers which involve communicating. Being good at communicating and at English is important for many jobs. In particular, communicating well in writing is crucial to anyone who has to give or receive instructions, write messages, letters or reports, argue a case – and so on. Spoken communication is also a keen feature in jobs that involve working with the media or the public. There are some kinds of work where being good at English is especially important if you are to be successful, and some where the use of English is an essential skill.

The various ways in which you can be 'good at English' include:

- **report writing** – writing English which is clear and accurate, but not necessarily creative;
- **creative English** – writing English in a particular personal style, or to produce a certain effect;
- **literary English and reading** – a critical interest in literature and books;
- **interpretation** – careful interpretation of oral or written language, perhaps to establish an exact meaning.

For each of these groups, here are some suggestions of the kinds of work which make particular use of that type of English.

Report writing
Many administrative jobs require you to be:

- able to express your own or other people's ideas in clear, concise language;

- good at spelling, grammar and sentence construction;
- good at choosing words and phrases which convey your meaning accurately.

Most of these jobs are for people with at least a good general education, while many are for graduates or professionally qualified people. Jobs include secretary, clerical or administrative assistant/officer, legal executive, solicitor, company secretary, journalist, technical author, information officer/scientist, publishing editors, public relations or press officer, together with all the professions and managerial jobs where written reports are often required, e.g. surveyors, architects, engineers, bank managers, industrialists.

Creative writing

Very few jobs allow you to write creatively, using your own personal style or manipulating words to produce certain ideas and images in the mind of the reader. Even in the jobs listed here, you may have to conform to 'house style' most of the time: journalism (newspapers, magazines, TV, radio); advertising and public relations; copywriting; authorship (novels, plays, speeches, articles, etc). You can also be involved in creative writing as an English teacher or primary teacher.

Interpretation

This covers the types of work where you need to interpret very carefully the meaning conveyed by language, either written or spoken, to establish the writer's or speaker's exact intended expression.

Possibilities include: barrister, solicitor, legal executive, conveyancer and others working with the law; archivist; historian; advice workers, for instance, in the Citizens' Advice Bureaux; consumer protection and law centre staff; market researchers and others who design and use questionnaires or oral interviews;

some computer personnel, such as systems analysts; designers, producing and working from clients' briefs; lexicographers; translators and interpreters; and writers, such as technical authors, who specialise in expressing difficult, technical terms in words that a lay person can understand.

WRITING FOR A LIVING

> A large number of people make their living through writing, and most of them are not involved in writing works of fiction, or indeed in writing books at all. The small number of authors whose names are household words, and who make millions from selling the film rights of their latest book, let alone the royalties, are balanced by all the many writers who never see their names in print.

Writing books

The chances of writing a best seller are not very high. Even well-known writers have often had many manuscripts rejected before they finally manage to get published. Many authors have other occupations as well, so that they don't rely on their earnings from writing for the whole of their income. Writers of academic and educational books often come into this category.

Authors are usually self-employed and earn a 'royalty' on each book that the publisher sells. Established authors usually get an 'advance' on a book so that they have some cash to live on while the book is being published. Many writers are experts on some particular subject, and may be approached by a publisher who sees an opening in the market for a new publication. An editor may decide that a new book about a particular subject is a good idea, and will select the best person to write the text.

Handling all the legal aspects of authorship can be complex. Many authors have a **literary agent** who handles this side of the business and will also help them to find a publisher for any new work they produce.

The most difficult area of authorship to break into is writing novels and children's fiction. It is easier to get into specialist writing of non-fiction books.

Scriptwriting

Scriptwriting for radio, television and film provides a good source of employment for writers, although breaking into the market is not easy. The BBC and other broadcasting organisations run occasional competitions to find new scriptwriting talent. Radio is perhaps the most hopeful market for new writing, simply because of the large output of drama and comedy produced.

Successful scriptwriters take a sound, creative idea and turn it into a saleable finished product. They need to be good at working to deadlines and producing material to order. To sell an idea for a script, they would produce a 'treatment', perhaps one episode of a series together with plot outlines for several others. It is quite a well-paid branch of the writing profession so long as you can go on producing the goods, which can be stressful. Payment is normally made through a one-off lump sum, rather than by royalties as in book publishing.

Freelance journalism

Many magazines and journals rely on **freelance writers** to fill their columns every week, and this provides a basic income for a lot of writers. Normally, they are expert in some subject and know where their expertise can be sold. Specialisms can be anything from analysing what goes on in Chinese politics, through farming to pigeon-fancying. Some freelancers start with a background in journalism, others develop an interest into a source of income. As with scriptwriting, the ability to meet deadlines and to be reliable is highly valued by commissioning editors.

Copywriting

Advertising copywriters produce the text for all sorts of adverts – television commercials, newspaper adverts and brochures and handouts of all types. They are normally employed by advertising agencies and work in a team with designers and account executives. They don't need the long-distance stamina of the book author, but must produce creative ideas under pressure. There are now some higher education courses in copywriting.

Technical writing

Technical writers produce technical manuals and information which is highly detailed and practical. They usually have an engineering or other technical background, and their work involves clarity and accuracy rather than creative flair.

Indexing

Indexers work usually on a freelance basis for publishers. When the author and publisher have arrived at the final version of a publication, it is sent to a professional indexer to produce the index. The indexer has to make decisions about which items should be indexed and ensure that all the page references are correct. This is a job requiring a logical and methodical approach and which usually involves the use of a computer.

Other jobs involving writing

Many jobs where the conveying of information is important involve writing. Producing this book involved a great deal of writing! Public relations and press officers are often involved in writing press releases and handouts. People in all sorts of jobs have to write reports and summaries as an important part of their work. These jobs rarely involve what you might call creative writing, but they do require the writers to express themselves clearly and concisely.

TRAINING TO BE A WRITER

There are some higher and further education courses in creative and technical writing, which can be helpful, e.g. contemporary writing, scriptwriting for film and television, and performance writing, as well as various part-time courses in many local colleges. Look in the various directories and compendia of courses in your local careers service library. Private courses advertised in the press tend to be expensive, and usually offer a rather exaggerated idea of possible earnings from writing! Practice, and reading a lot of other people's work, are extremely useful activities.

More detailed descriptions of these and many other occupations are contained within this book.

JOURNALISM

Journalists gather information about what is going on in the world, and write reports for publication in newspapers and magazines and to be read on radio and television. Some are general journalists reporting on the whole range of local, national and international events. Others specialise in areas such as sport, foreign news, politics, court and social events, fashion and cookery, holidays and travel and gardening. You can start training with good GCSEs or their equivalent.

A journalist needs:
- an interest in local, national and international affairs;
- an ability to write in a style that is interesting to read and easy to understand;
- good grammar, spelling and punctuation;
- a genuine interest in people, and good social skills;
- a willingness to work irregular hours and to put the needs of the job before a social life;
- an ability to work under pressure to meet deadlines.

The main areas of employment for journalists are the local daily and weekly newspapers, the national press, news agencies, the vast range of periodicals published weekly and monthly, and, of course, radio and television.

Newspaper journalism
The main employer of new entrants is the provincial press.

Here, **trainee journalists** can learn the basic skills under less pressure than on the national papers (though woe betide the local reporter who gets the Little Snoring gymkhana results wrong, or pairs off the wrong couple on the wedding photographs page!). There is little chance of moving into the national press until you have three years' experience as a **qualified journalist** on a provincial paper, and have proved your skills and reliability. However, specialist writers are recruited from different backgrounds.

Many journalists start their careers in local newspapers and move on to senior positions and editorship, without wanting to break into positions on the quality national press. But, whether you stay or move on, local journalism is a vital training ground for any new entrant. Some provincial papers take on trainee journalists, while others recruit trainees from the pre-entry courses (see below). Some papers recruit graduates, who presently form over 50 per cent of new entrants.

The essence of good journalism is being able to fit in with the newspaper or magazine 'house style', in order to produce what the editor wants – a paper which the public will buy, and in which local and national firms will buy advertising space. The profit in local papers comes mainly from advertising revenue, and it is the *sole* income source for free newspapers.

Journalism can be an interesting career, but it certainly takes hard work and dedication to get on.

> ### Clare – junior reporter on a local newspaper
> ' It was hard to get my first job in journalism, as there are so many well-qualified people going for the same jobs. I think I only got my apprenticeship by impressing the editor with my knowledge of current affairs and of his newspaper. I'd gone to the library and

read as many back copies as I could, and I'd watched all the news programmes on TV so that I was as up to date as I could be.

I had to start at the bottom, covering events such as weddings and flower shows, but now I have passed the National Council for the Training of Journalists' foundation course (12 weeks on block release), I have been moved on to cover news stories, which I prefer. I love "getting a story". I'm naturally nosy and like to ask questions all the time. The difficult bit is writing it all up afterwards, not only to make it interesting, but also to make it fit into the small space the editor has given me! It's not easy, writing in a very noisy office with people shouting and running around, all trying to beat deadlines. Deadlines mean that I have learnt to write very, very fast and have developed my own version of shorthand as well as keyboard skills. What I love most of all, once I've sweated over a piece, is seeing my name in print. It's worth all the hard work and all the long hours just for that.

Of course, news stories don't just happen between the hours of nine to five. Some of the most interesting ones happen in the middle of the night or at the weekend, but I don't mind so long as the story is a good one!

I hope eventually to win promotion to sub-editor, where I could re-write stories and do the headlines and layout, but I think I might miss the travelling around that I get to do now. However, at the moment, I am happy being a junior reporter as every day is different.

PRE-ENTRY COURSES

There are special one-year, full-time pre-entry courses in journalism at several colleges, which provide basic training. Over 300 people a year enter newspaper journalism this way. For entry to a full-time course, you will need a minimum of five GCSEs at grade C, including English, or their equivalent, although in practice colleges may ask for two A levels, a BTEC National qualification, or an Advanced GNVQ. This entry requirement may be waived for mature applicants. Applications are made directly to the National Council for the Training of Journalists (NCTJ), and, when writing for an application form, it is essential to send a stamped, addressed envelope (23cm x 10cm). All applicants to pre-entry courses take written tests in English, story and essay writing, general knowledge and current affairs. Those who pass this hurdle are then interviewed.

Awards for these courses are discretionary and you must make an application to your Local Education Authority. A handful of newspaper companies sponsor trainees on pre-entry courses.

DIRECT ENTRY

The newspaper journalism training scheme for direct entrants under 24 is controlled by the National Council for the Training of Journalists. Accreditation of the modules can lead to NVQs up to level 4. Application should be made direct to the editor of any local or regional newspaper. Those who are successful serve a six-month probationary period, followed by a two-year qualifying period, during which NCTJ examinations are taken. Training and further education is carried out in colleges and company training centres accredited by the NCTJ, or through a distance learning pack. The minimum educational requirements are five GCSEs at grade C, or their equivalent; or one A level plus four different GCSEs at grade C; or two A levels/

Advanced GNVQ/BTEC National Diploma, plus two GCSEs at grade C. Only about 5 per cent of accepted trainees have only GCSE or equivalent qualifications.

Some newspaper groups and companies have their own in-company training schemes to meet the NCTJ requirements. These include Southern Newspapers and Midland News Association.

GRADUATE ENTRY

Direct entry graduates should apply to editors of local or regional papers. Successful applicants serve a probationary six months, followed by a further two-year qualifying period. During this time, trainees attend an eight-week block release course at an NCTJ-approved college. Graduates can apply to company training schemes, but are also considered for the one-year full-time pre-entry courses described above. Additionally, for graduates of other disciplines, there are one-year postgraduate diploma courses in journalism at various universities. There is a reduced qualifying period of eighteen months if you have completed one of these.

Relevant degrees, etc – Various colleges offer degrees in subjects such as communication and media studies, which could be of interest but which *do not provide journalism training as such*. A dedicated journalism degree course will offer units in media law, shorthand, public affairs (including local and national government) and the basic skills of journalistic writing and ethics.

It is possible to study for an HND in Business Studies with a journalism option. MAs can be taken at a number of universities.

Adults: entrants between 24 and 30 are required to follow a programme of training agreed between their employer and the

NCTJ. There is no formal training requirement for entrants over 30. Adults can apply for the pre-entry courses mentioned above, for in-company training schemes, or for the postgraduate courses, with appropriate work experience.

Would I like it?

- A job in this area means you need to be able to write, and perhaps speak, well.
- An interest in a specialist subject such as history, science, English, music or foreign languages, will be useful.
- You will probably enjoy finding out about things and about people.

- You will have an interest in working or dealing with all sorts of people.
- Many of the jobs involve working under pressure, with deadlines to meet.
- Some of the work is physically tiring, with long periods of standing.
- You may have to work at weekends or in the evenings.
- You need to be a very accurate and thorough sort of person.

Magazines

Every year, between 400 and 500 people start their careers on some of the 4000 periodicals published in Britain. There are two main types of periodical: about 2000 professional, trade and technical periodicals, and a similar number of magazines for leisure reading – generally called consumer magazines. Possibly 300 of the 2000 consumer magazines are nationally known, including women's weeklies and monthlies, family weeklies, teenage papers, children's comics, hobby and leisure magazines.

The work on periodicals is similar to newspaper journalism, although the news-gathering covers a narrower field, and there are proportionally more specialists and sub-editors. **Periodical journalists** need two particular skills – journalistic ability, and a special understanding of their readers and the subjects they are writing about. This can be a demanding combination, especially when it involves complex subjects in the trade, technical and business field – such as medicine, law, science and technology. Here, graduates and other specialists are required. Generally, educational requirements for new entrants are the same as for newspapers.

Besides permanent staff jobs, there are also considerable opportunities for freelancers to write articles. Additionally, there is scope for people with experience in another field to enter periodical journalism, writing about their own specialisms.

Freelancers can gain membership of the National Union of Journalists or Institute of Journalists.

You can enter periodical journalism as a direct entrant, or following a one-year pre-entry course. For the pre-entry course you need a minimum of two A levels plus two GCSEs at grade C including English, or the equivalent (this may be waived for mature applicants). If you wish to apply as a direct entrant, select some suitable periodicals and write to the editors concerned, briefly outlining your education, special abilities and interests, and why you want to work on their publication. Enclose any relevant examples of your own writing. Before any interviews, it is vital to study that particular magazine beforehand so that you can talk intelligently about it.

Many new entrants join periodicals and magazines for a trial period of three to six months. During and after that time, your main training will be on-the-job. This should be supplemented with external training courses approved by the Periodicals Training Council (PTC). Some of the larger publishing groups provide in-company training as a substitute for, or as a supplement to, PTC-approved courses.

News agencies

News agencies provide a service to the national press by covering events worldwide. The daily press cannot afford to pay to have a correspondent in every place in the world where news items might be gathered. News agencies, such as Reuters, provide a basic service which can be supplemented by foreign correspondents. Agency staff are always experienced journalists.

Radio and television

This is a sought-after area where there has been expansion, but which is currently fairly stable. Entry is very competitive. Local radio tends to recruit journalists with a local press training and good microphone manner and voice, but there are also pre-entry and postgraduate courses for intending **radio journalists**.

Possibilities also exist for really keen young entrants with appropriate experience of basic sound techniques, e.g. through hospital or college radio stations, but persistence will be called for. A demonstration tape of an interview or report could be very helpful.

BBC radio and TV recruit *trained* journalists to work in their newsrooms. There is also a news trainee scheme, mainly for graduates, which offers two years' training in broadcasting news techniques. ITN also trains a few graduates each year, but relies mainly on recruiting experienced staff. Contact broadcasting companies directly, for further details of their schemes.

Teletext is an expanding area offering increasing opportunities for journalists. Companies usually employ experienced journalists. However, Ceefax occasionally train a new entrant without journalistic experience.

Researchers

Most television companies prefer graduates. Many researchers, especially those working in current affairs, have a journalistic background or previous experience in radio or television. Direct entrants into the BBC usually complete a two-year training period based in London. ITV recruit few direct entrants into research. Some larger stations may have their own training courses.

TECHNICAL WRITING

> Technical writers or authors are the people responsible for writing technical leaflets, handbooks, sales brochures, development reports, operating instructions, training manuals, and so on. Most opportunities are in the areas of engineering, computing and electronics. Technical writers have a good background knowledge of the subject they are writing about, plus an ability to write in clear, concise English.

If you've just bought a stereo, you will need operating instructions and specifications of its performance. Repair technicians need much more detail, including circuit diagrams and component numbers for all the transistors, capacitors and resistors in the amplifier.

An aircraft requires volumes of technical literature to enable maintenance engineers to do all the necessary work on it. The engineers need to know:

- the colour coding on the miles of wiring in the electric systems;
- all the measurements and tolerances of the mechanical and hydraulic systems;
- the checks for wear and fatigue that must be made.

The job of the technical writer, no matter what the subject or level, *always* includes:

- finding out what the reader needs to know;

- obtaining the information required;
- preparing a draft of the text and commissioning any artwork required;
- finalising information text and illustrations, and obtaining the necessary approvals;
- presenting the final layout in a form that can be easily read by the user.

Technical authors often work as a team, particularly on large and complex projects. Information is gathered from many different sources, and is then organised and classified. Drawings must be commissioned from technical illustrators, photographs may be required, and outside component manufacturers may need to be consulted. There is also freelance work available.

There are three main areas of employment:

Technical publication agencies or consultancies – they usually undertake to produce a finished product and employ their own writers and illustrators. They may also act as agents, supplying writers to work under contract with a large firm's technical publications department.

Publication departments of manufacturing firms – large firms like Shell or ICI have their own technical writing departments.

Public and government departments – organisations like the Ministry of Defence, the BBC and British Telecom also have substantial technical publications departments.

What it takes

For most of the available work, technical authors must have a good understanding of engineering principles and, preferably, specialised knowledge of one or more fields such as electronics, computing or hydraulics. They need to be able to understand engineering drawings and circuit diagrams. Experience of areas like quality control, inspection, installation and servicing can be a great help.

They must be able to express themselves clearly, concisely and unambiguously in writing. There is very little scope for 'creative' writing. Descriptions must be written in a very straightforward style, and in language that will be understood by the likely reader. Authors also need to be good at interviewing people, tactfully and patiently, to get the information that they need.

TRAINING

There are three main training routes:

- A **degree** in mechanical, production, electronic and electrical engineering, or physics, followed by a postgraduate qualification. This is mainly for high-level electronic work. There are a few postgraduate courses in technical authorship. There is a specific degree in technical communication which covers written and graphical information and electronic documents, interactive videos and similar techniques.
- **BTEC Higher National Certificate or Diploma** in combination with practical experience, for example as a test or maintenance engineer.
- **City & Guilds courses** 536/1 Technical Communication Techniques and 536/2 Technical Authorship are offered at various further education colleges. You can also study for these courses through private organisations or by correspondence. About thirty organisations offer these and other college-based or distance learning courses – contact the Institute of Scientific and Technical Communicators for a full list.

It may be possible to enter the field of technical writing as A level, Advanced GNVQ or BTEC National Certificate/

Diploma holders, direct from school or college. This is not a usual method of entry but, with some firms, it may be possible to be taken on as a trainee to gain practical experience while studying for a BTEC Higher National.

WORKING IN LIBRARIES & INFORMATION SERVICES

> Library and information work involves working with books, computer databases and with all the other modern methods of storing information. There is work for highly qualified professionals and more routine work for library assistants.

Library and information work is a career about which people think they know quite a lot. There's the TV stereotype character – bespectacled, fumbling and shy, working in a dull, dusty place. But it's hardly a typical or accurate picture of modern librarians or information officers and their place of work!

Some misconceptions

There are perhaps four main misunderstandings about working in libraries and information services.

'Librarians are people who check your books in and out of the library, and put all the returned books back on the shelves.'
In fact, two main types of staff work in libraries – chartered librarians and information professionals, and library assistants. These are quite different jobs (though in very small libraries there is more overlap). Library assistants normally see to the routine running of the library. Librarians and information specialists are highly qualified professionals whose duties are described below.

'Librarians and assistants spend all of their time with books.'
This is no longer the case. Books are just one means of storing information so that it can be found again. In public libraries, cassettes, CDs, and videos are all part of the library stock. Increasingly, systems other than print are used for storing information. Computers and viewdata systems are used very frequently to find information. Pages of print can be microfilmed to be viewed through an enlarger when required. These applications of new technology mean that information can be stored much more economically and found much more rapidly and efficiently; it is possible to access information on computers all over the world!

'Library and information work is a good career for someone who doesn't like mixing with other people.'
Not true at all! To be a good provider of information, you have to get on with people, understand their requirements and be able to communicate clearly. You also have to cope with grumblers and people who cannot articulate their enquiries very well.

'Most librarians work in public libraries.'
These are the only libraries and information services that many people know about, apart from school and college libraries and resource centres. But in fact, whereas not long ago at least half of all librarians worked in public libraries, they now account for only 28 per cent of members of the Library Association. There is increasing employment for librarians in other sectors of the economy, wherever there are information needs.

Where library and information professionals work

Besides public lending libraries, the other main types of libraries are:

- public reference libraries and information services – often a department of the public library (as is the lending library), but may be housed in a separate library building;

- academic libraries in universities, colleges, etc;
- the national libraries;
- special libraries and information services for industry, commerce, government departments, etc;
- libraries in schools;
- libraries in hospitals, prisons, etc.

Academic libraries in universities, colleges, and research institutes contain many specialist academic books, periodicals, documents and databases. Each subject division is usually staffed by specialists. An academic librarian is very involved with the resourcing of courses, authorising loans from other libraries and assisting students in finding the information they need.

The national libraries include the British Library, the National Library of Scotland, the National Library of Wales and the National Art Library. They are huge libraries of great importance, with many specialist subject staff.

Specialist libraries and information services, which serve particular groups of users, include the House of Commons library, BBC libraries, newspapers, government departments, scientific research organisations, architectural and legal practices, etc. Big companies have financial libraries, major hospitals have medical libraries, and industries have libraries containing all the specialist information on the technologies, raw materials and processes which they use. Special libraries may hold textual, musical and pictorial materials in the form of pamphlets, periodicals, research reports, musical scores, microfilms, videodiscs, compact discs and subscribe to on-line databases, etc. The collections may be small, with the librarian or information officer also spending some time working as a researcher.

School and college libraries are found in technical, agricultural, music and art colleges. Schools may just offer library assistant or clerical assistant posts, but, in most areas, secondary school and college libraries are managed by fully qualified professional staff.

What do library and information professionals do?

The work of librarians (or information officers) and their assistants varies a lot, according to where they are employed.

They **select** books, periodicals, magazines, cassettes and other materials. They must carefully balance the needs of their users against the available resources. In a public or general interest library, an awareness of local tastes, authors, subjects and publishers is essential to achieve greatest effect. In the public library service, library and information staff often choose books and other materials as a team, sharing their knowledge. In a special or academic library, the users may influence decisions on which items are to be bought.

They do **research** for information to help users solve a particular problem. The librarian or information officer uses reference books, bibliographies, periodicals and magazines, computer databases or any other available source to provide the best possible answer to the person making the enquiry. This detective work can be a great source of job satisfaction, and forms a high proportion of the work in all types of libraries. In a public library, the enquiries can be very wide-ranging: helping children with homework topics, adults undertaking independent learning or doing quizzes and competitions or wanting information on foreign countries, local authors researching historical information, etc. In academic and special libraries, complex enquiries are likely to need a good knowledge of the subject and bring the librarian into contact with other special information collections, using all kinds of new technology.

The librarian or information officer in an academic or a special library may be involved in the **cataloguing** and classification of materials. This is to determine where items should be housed within the library, and to store information about them in a catalogue (probably on a computer) so that they can be efficiently traced and retrieved when information is required. This is not a significant part of the work for many staff in a modern public library, as it tends to be done at the library headquarters on behalf of all the libraries in the area; or libraries may buy in a cataloguing service from a major library system supplier.

Specialist librarians could be involved in classifying and cataloguing individual collections of books, art works, music, etc, perhaps for an auction house or an insurance company.

They **compile** bibliographies – in academic libraries, a typical task is compiling lists of books and other materials on specific topics, in response to requests.

They **manage** the library, information service or resource centre, its staff, contents and systems.

They tell people about the library or information service, and **promote** its services and stock, **displaying** that stock to best effect. They **help** library users to find the book they require and **organise** an efficient reservation service for readers to reserve particular materials they want. They also **prepare** packs of relevant information on specific subjects such as bereavement, setting up a small business, etc.

Librarians in the public library and information service may be involved in **working with the community** – providing space for (and organising) exhibitions, cultural activities, meetings, talks, poetry readings, children's story sessions and other activities during school holidays. As part of their community services, public librarians look after the needs of elderly and housebound people through Books on Wheels, disabled and disadvantaged people through Talking Books for the Blind, special books for readers with learning difficulties, and large-print books for those with sight problems. They also make special provision for ethnic minorities and other special groups.

What makes a good library and information professional?

Whilst a love of books is an asset and most librarians enjoy reading, these qualities are not essential for the job. There are many other qualities which are more important.

They include:

- being able to deal with all kinds of people in a pleasant, tactful and efficient manner without getting flustered;
- having a lively interest in searching out information, whatever the format, to satisfy enquirers in all types of libraries and information services – including retrieving information from computer databases;
- being able to organise one's own work and that of the staff, to achieve efficiency;
- having a wide general knowledge, some familiarity with foreign languages, an interest in current events and a reliable memory. A good visual memory is important for the librarian of an art collection;
- being prepared to work shifts, in most public and academic libraries – not minding having to work some evenings and some Saturdays, as these are the times most convenient to many users;
- being reasonably physically fit – important in a job which may keep you on your feet

TRAINING

Professional library and information work is an all-graduate profession. There are two main ways of training and either route is acceptable for work in the public library service. For some specialist and academic library posts, the second route may be preferred:

- A degree in library/information studies, taken singly or as a joint honours degree with another subject. This qualifies for a mandatory award.
- A degree in any subject followed by a full-time or part-time postgraduate course in library/information studies or information science. Bursaries and studentships for full-time postgraduate courses are very few and must be applied for through the academic institution offering the course. You should get some practical experience in a library or information-related job before a postgraduate course, particularly if applying for a bursary or studentship. Usually, nine months' to a year's work experience is required; details of some temporary positions are available from the Library Association from October to July. Degree-level qualifications are required for admission to postgraduate courses.

Minimum requirements for degree courses are usually two A levels/Advanced GNVQ/BTEC National Diploma, plus supporting GCSEs. You will need English language GCSE at grade C or equivalent; a foreign language and a science are useful.

Mature entrants may be accepted onto some degree courses without the usual entry qualifications, as previous experience and knowledge are taken into account.

There are information posts in some organisations which can be entered by graduates without professional qualifications, but your career would be limited if you were not fully qualified. Most library and information professionals belong to the Library Association, the chartered professional body in the UK. To satisfy the Library Association's criteria for admission to its professional Register of Chartered Members, most candidates will have successfully completed a degree or postgraduate course accredited by the Association, followed by a minimum of one year's approved training while in a first professional post. Graduates without library and information qualifications can also apply for admission to the Register after completing a longer period of professional experience.

For further information and a list of courses, write to the Library Association.

Library assistant

Library assistants help run libraries. Their job involves:

- issuing books and other materials to borrowers, often using a computer system;
- checking returned items and putting them back on the shelves;
- helping people to find books and information;
- sending reminders to borrowers who keep books and other materials too long;
- informing people that items they have requested have arrived;
- helping with filing and other administrative and clerical work;
- dealing with enquiries.

Library assistants can work in any type of library mentioned above, including mobile library vans. To be good at the work, you need to get on well with all sorts of people, and to be patient and not easily flustered by sudden rushes of work or difficult customers. A good memory helps, and a liking for dealing with information. 'Awkward', but not always unpopular, hours are often entailed, with some evening/weekend work. There is often scope for part-time work.

Chris – library assistant in a public library

❝ I became interested in library work when my mum persuaded me to go for a Saturday job in our public library. I had found it difficult to get any Saturday work at all, but didn't particularly want to work in a library. However, I needed the money and was desperate! I had no idea the work would be so interesting, and I became hooked from then on.

My Saturday job helped me to get a full-time job, once I had left school with a reasonable array of GCSEs. I had direct experience to offer, and knew what the job was all about. What I like about the work is the fact that every day is different. I sometimes deal directly with the public, issuing and receiving books and taking money for fines on overdue ones. I really like helping people to find something on the shelves, as I can then show off my knowledge of the library! Now I've been here a while, I have got to know the regulars and the types of book they enjoy, although sometimes they surprise me with their choice. I use the microfiche and the computer database when people want more detailed information.

Filling the shelves, and tidying up after people have left books and magazines on the tables, are not quite so interesting, but I don't really mind. I find it fascinating to see what people have been reading! I'm being trained "on-the-job", and hope to get some National Vocational Qualifications under my belt. ❞

EDUCATION AND TRAINING

Educational requirements are usually a minimum of four GCSEs at grade C, with English being the most important subject. The basic duties are learned on-the-job, but you can also take a one-year, part-time or distance learning City & Guilds Library and Information Competencies Certificate. The BTEC National Certificate of Achievement in Library and Information Work is a double unit which can be taken alone (approximately one-year part-time) or as part of a National Certificate in Business and Finance, which takes two years part-time. These qualifications may soon also count towards a National Vocational Qualification, but it is unlikely that NVQs will eliminate the need for a degree to achieve professional status.

Vacancies for library assistants can be found in local newspapers and, occasionally, in the *Library Association Record Vacancies Supplement*, which is sent out only to members of the Association.

Promotion opportunities are rather limited, though there are posts for Senior Library Assistants in larger libraries. The Library Association produces an information booklet on job-hunting for members.

just THE JOB

INFORMATION OFFICER

> Information officers are people who enjoy delving for information and communicating it to others. They are fact-finders, fact-researchers and fact-communicators. They work in industry, commerce and public sector organisations. Most, but not all, are graduates.

Employers of information officers include information bureaux, consumer advice centres, the national offices of the Citizens' Advice Bureau, government departments, the BBC, the National Trust, English Heritage, the Forestry Commission, bodies such as the Arts Council, charities, tourist information offices, museums, newspapers, research bodies, the careers service and, of course, public, reference, and specialist libraries.

Jobs tend to be based in larger towns and cities, and not all posts have the title *information officer*. Other terms used for similar kinds of work include research officer, education officer, publications officer and publicity officer. Many information/research officers work for government information services as press officers. Others work in publicity, writing and editing booklets and leaflets, organising conferences and exhibitions, and producing TV and radio commercials. All central government departments require information officers, as do public organisations all over the country.

What do information officers do?
The sort of work undertaken varies considerably from one post to another. In some posts, the emphasis is on public relations

work, in others it is on publications. Information officers would:

- **collect** up-to-date information by research, from books, the media, periodicals, and other sources;
- **catalogue and store** it so that it is accessible when required;
- **share** it with, and publicise it to, enquirers and colleagues who are likely to be interested;
- **produce reports**, leaflets, news items, reviews, etc.

Would I like it?

- the work is often varied and almost always busy and changing;
- you need to be both curious and patient;
- you also need to be approachable, helpful, and good at communicating with users of your service, whether members of the public or your colleagues;
- you should be well organised, so that your information sources are at your fingertips;
- adaptability is needed to make use of new ways of classifying information, and of changes in technology – such as computers and microprocessors – which greatly improve storage and retrieval of information;
- a good memory is an asset – not because you have to store masses of information in your head, but because you do need to know how to track down information sources as quickly as possible. It helps if you have the sort of mind which retains useful snippets, so that you can say, *'I know I've read something about that recently . . .'* and then find the article!

BECOMING AN INFORMATION OFFICER

Information officers come from a wide variety of backgrounds. Some are trained librarians or information scientists. Some are experienced specialists or professionals in a particular field who have moved into information as a career development – journalists, for example. This change is quite common, as their training in sniffing out information is particularly useful. Others may be civil servants or local government staff, who have branched out into information work. Some have previously worked in clerical, secretarial and administrative posts. Public relations work, publicity, personnel, teaching and other careers that combine dealing with facts and dealing with people, can also provide suitable backgrounds.

IS THERE A 'BEST' WAY TO GET STARTED?

Many information posts are for people with degrees or equivalent-level qualifications. Secretarial abilities are sometimes asked for, and a specialised knowledge gained through another job may prove useful.

This is not really a career for a school-leaver or college-leaver. You would need either relevant experience or training, or both, before being considered for most information posts. The most suitable training to aim for would be a degree or postgraduate qualification in library and information studies, for which you would require two or three A levels/Advanced GNVQ, together with supporting GCSEs at grade C (or equivalent). Alternatively, at postgraduate level, a degree in any discipline is acceptable. But, as mentioned above, this is by no means the only way in.

Some typical job advertisements

To give you some idea of the variety of posts which occur, here are some extracts from job vacancy advertisements.

Assistant information officer – *'Major London advertising agency seeks enthusiastic assistant in library. Similar work experience essential, especially in filing and general office routine.'*

Publicity and information officer – *'for arts association, to provide technical and secretarial support to the Press and Publicity Officer by preparing copy and supervising design and print production, particularly with the Association's lively newspaper. Also to assist in the establishment of an information bank on arts facilities in London. Initiative and ability to write copy and type, together with a willingness to share office routines, are essential.'*

Teacher/publicist for museum – *'Work includes giving talks, dealing with enquiries, compiling worksheets, advising teachers on using the museum's resources, preparing and distributing publicity literature. Candidates must have a degree, a teaching qualification and at least one year's teaching experience. Interest in publicity work essential – experience an advantage.'*

National Trust regional information officer – *'Duties include publicity, press, radio and TV, public relations, functions, events, open days, lectures, members' associations, membership recruiting, fund-raising, publications, exhibitions and display, interpretation, education and youth activities. Previous experience in some part of this work is essential, together with the ability to work in a team of several disciplines.'*

Publications officer – *'Responsible for the production of a variety of publications, maintenance of a small reference library and the provision of a general enquiry and public relations service. It offers scope to develop an interest in publishing, requiring an intelligent and creative approach to information-handling. Post for a graduate.'*

INFORMATION SCIENTIST

> Information scientists work mainly in the libraries of industrial, commercial or research organisations, for government departments and in other specialist libraries and information units. Information science is a graduate profession.

Information is one of the principal products of the twentieth century. A flood of books, magazines, journals and papers pours out of the world's printing presses every day, and every year the torrent grows. This quantity of material can be overwhelming to users. Add to this all the data now on electronic media and the need for people with the training and expertise to deal with information becomes apparent.

Information scientists, unlike **information officers**, have scientific or technical expertise in a specific area such as engineering, law or pharmaceuticals. Information scientists make greater use of information technology to research and retrieve current data for a particular company, client or service. Information officers assist clients in accessing their own information.

There is a lot of overlap between the professions **librarian** and **information scientist** (particularly in special libraries where the jobs are often combined). Traditionally, librarians select, organise and classify information to make it accessible. The special expertise of information scientists was in using information collections to answer complex queries and to meet the information requirements of their organisation. Nowadays, the training for the work is much the same, and both jobs may carry out a full range of information tasks, whatever the job title.

Information scientists must have a thorough understanding of classifying and indexing systems, so that materials and information can be retrieved when required. Nowadays it is vital to know how to access computer databases, linking into computer systems all over the world, on occasions. *Designing* information systems is a specialism in its own right, a field into which information scientists and librarians may move.

Information scientists answer all sorts of complex enquiries and queries, by searching indexes, records, files and databases for material, and deciding what sort of reply to provide – a brief outline or a highly detailed report.

Some typical jobs include:

- compiling economic reports on a country where a sales drive is projected;
- summarising recently published research concerning a particular chemical process;
- doing a literature survey relating to a topic in astrophysics.

Scientists and professional people often have little time to read everything new which is relevant to their subject. The information scientist provides them with a very useful and important service, by selecting and editing material from journals, periodicals, books, etc, and producing summaries to draw their attention to potentially valuable information. Computers are again used here, to store 'profiles' of the requirements of individuals, to make a rapid match with information held on the contents of publications.

Job vacancies are advertised in the national quality daily newspapers, *New Scientist* and the *Times Higher Educational*

Supplement, and in specialist journals. Members of the Library Association and the Institute of Information Scientists are sent regular vacancy bulletins. Some information scientists opt to work in publishing, with organisations which produce abstracts, journals or scientific/technical periodicals. Here, there are writing and editing posts which may require specialist subject knowledge.

TRAINING

Information science is a profession for well-qualified graduates. To start with, therefore, you will need at least five GCSEs at grade C (to include English, and preferably mathematics, at least one science and a foreign language) and two or more A levels/Advanced GNVQ, and, at postgraduate level, a degree. There are two main training routes.

- There are first degrees in library and/or information science/management which include the study of retrieval methods, computing, scientific and language studies.
- Alternatively, you could first take a degree or equivalent qualification, ideally in a science, social science, economics or business studies, and then follow this with a full-time or part-time postgraduate course in library and/or information science. Other disciplines (non-scientific) are also often acceptable. Work experience as an assistant in a library or information unit is often required in order to be accepted for a postgraduate course, but at first degree level is only necessary if you are studying part-time or by distance learning.

Mature entry for adults is possible, but is really restricted to those with a relevant background in science, technology, computing or a similar area. Mature graduates can be favoured, as the work is best performed by well-educated people with skills in management, communication and technology.

It is not easy to say which is the best route into information science. Some jobs require a good academic background in a particular discipline but, for others, a specialist library and information studies degree or postgraduate qualification may be more appropriate. One point to consider is that library and information studies first degrees normally entitle students to a mandatory award, whereas there is fierce competition for (and no automatic entitlement to) awards for full-time postgraduate courses. Careers services at universities can offer guidance to undergraduates and graduates.

just THE JOB

ARCHIVIST

> An archivist's main job is the care of written and other records, ancient and modern. Over half of British archivists work in local authorities, with the rest in businesses and other organisations which keep records, such as cathedrals, historic houses and museums. Most archivists are graduates with postgraduate qualifications.

Archivists work with records originating either from institutions or from individuals, which can be used in a variety of ways. Archives may consist of written material, audiotapes and videotapes, films, photographs, and even computer tapes and discs. Archive materials are unique and irreplaceable, and are usually kept in strongrooms to which the public does not have access.

There are many archives throughout the UK, comprising both public and private material. These include:

- **the national archives** – held in the Public Record Office in London, consisting of millions of documents from the Domesday Book onwards;
- **local government records** – records of all the things for which local government bodies are responsible; information inherited from other long-dead authorities, such as workhouse guardians and school boards; collections obtained from private sources;
- **ecclesiastical archives** – great collections in the cathedrals, and registers of baptisms, marriages and burials in parish churches.

The types of records which might be preserved include:

- legal and government records;
- records of industrial and commercial organisations and activities;
- ecclesiastical records;
- aristocratic family records;
- records illustrating the social history of people from all walks of life.

What do archivists do?

- They collect, select and catalogue archives.
- They make their records available to users, and must be able to guide them to the right documents, so it is important that they are good communicators.
- They use computers to produce catalogues, guides, lists and indexes of their archive material. Preparing lectures, exhibitions and educational material, and helping and advising researchers, are also part of the job.
- They must also destroy records, because, like libraries, many archives are still being added to. Not everything can or should be kept, so archivists must often decide what should be disposed of and what preserved.
- They preserve archives. They must understand the physical properties of materials in their care and provide the necessary conditions for their survival.

TRAINING

Archivists need an academic background, and it helps if they are knowledgeable about social and political history and economics. They need to be able to read handwriting from all periods, to be competent in Latin and to have some knowledge of such things as heraldry and land law. They must be accurate and methodical and, incidentally, prepared to work in dusty and

dirty conditions — not all archives are kept in modern air-conditioned buildings.

It may be possible to start a career as an **archive assistant**, directly after higher education or with A levels or equivalent. Normally, however, archivists start after a one-year postgraduate course in archive administration, offered at some universities and recognised by the Society of Archivists. Preferred first degree subjects are history, classics, English, languages or law. Applicants who have done some voluntary vacation work in a local authority record office will have an advantage at selection.

EMPLOYMENT

More than half of the archivists in Britain work for local government, in museums, record offices or libraries. An increasing number are now working in industry or commerce, where they may be concerned with recent records.

It is not generally very highly paid work, though industrial posts pay better than local or central government ones, or the universities.

just THE JOB

PUBLISHING

Publishing is a highly competitive business where sound editorial skills, commercial judgement, marketing and advertising skills are vital for survival. Although many graduates enter publishing, there are also opportunities for those with fewer qualifications.

Book publishing
Commissioning editor

When people talk about going into publishing, the job of a commissioning editor is the one they imagine themselves doing. These editors decide whether or not to publish a particular book – a job requiring considerable knowledge and judgement. Part of their role is to negotiate with authors and their agents about contracts, royalties and advances. Although making decisions about possible publications is their main role, commissioning editors need the background experience of copy editing.

Specialist and non-fiction books are largely commissioned. This means that, rather than a manuscript being submitted out of the blue by an author for a publisher's inspection, a commissioning editor with a particular idea in mind finds a suitable author to write the text. Ideas also come from authors who submit a synopsis of a work for consideration before writing it. In either case, the publisher usually agrees to publish the book before it ever reaches completed manuscript stage.

Fiction is almost always written speculatively – an author offers a finished novel to publishers, possibly through a literary agent, in the hope of getting it accepted.

Copy editor

Copy editors are responsible for the editing and proof-reading work which goes into getting texts ready for typesetting. Copy editors consult with production and design departments on the form a book will take, and may liaise with authors and their agents about layouts, proofs and cover design, etc. Organising ability is essential to be able to coordinate several jobs at once, and a good command of English is vital.

Production and design

This department is responsible for the design and manufacture of books, turning the author's and editor's work into something that can be sold.

Design work for books includes the page layout and type-specification as well as illustrations, and may be undertaken by the firm's own staff, or may be put out to freelancers or design studios. Most text and artwork origination now involves using computers (see next section). The actual printing and binding is normally carried out by a commercial printer, but the production director supervises costing, print-buying, scheduling and quality. It is necessary to be very organised and to be able to understand technical matters which may be raised by the printers. Production staff may be trained printers, graphic artists, possibly graduates recruited straight from college and trained on-the-job, or those who have taken appropriate diploma courses.

Marketing

To make a profit, publishers need to be able to sell books. To do this, they need to know what kinds of books are in demand. The business of marketing covers:

Sales – sales staff work as publishers' representatives, both in the UK and overseas, visiting booksellers and other outlets such as schools and colleges (educational publishers' representatives are often trained teachers). This job may well lead to sales management or a marketing post.

Promotion – this involves ensuring that the attention of the public, and of reviewers, is drawn to new books, through displays, authors' signing sessions, radio and TV interviews, etc. The job requires advertising and public relations skills. Marketing people often write promotional material.

Rights – this involves selling subsidiary rights to serialise and translate books, to re-issue books for bookclubs, to adapt texts for film, TV, stage and radio productions.

Other posts

There are occasional posts for researchers for reference works, though this work can be done by editorial assistants. The majority of opportunities in any publishing concern are in the support services, such as finance, personnel, computer services, distribution and general administration. These positions are very similar to their counterparts in industry/commerce and require appropriate training.

Alice – marketing coordinator

❝ I work as a marketing coordinator in the busy sales department of a publishing company.

I started off doing work experience for the company after finishing my degree. From there, I got a job as customer services coordinator and marketing assistant and have recently been promoted to marketing coordinator.

As the sales department is fairly small, my job is very varied. I also have more responsibility than someone in my position in a larger company might have.

A major part of my job is project-managing the production of the catalogues, brochures and adverts which promote our books. This involves writing copy, briefing designers and organising the printing and mailing of this marketing material. In addition, I control the budgets for all these projects to make sure that we don't spend money which we haven't got!

As well as this, I write and mail press releases, send out and follow up review copies of books and arrange reader offers in newspapers and magazines as well as keeping our marketing database up to date.

Although our department is small, it's also busy and I have to be very organised. We're always working to deadlines and I'm often juggling lots of projects at the same time. It's essential that I know what is most important and should be done first, but I also have to be flexible enough to drop everything when something unexpected and urgent crops up.

In my work with designers and printers from outside the company, I need tact and negotiating skills to make sure we get what we want, when we want it and at the right price.

The good thing about my job is that I'm gaining skills which I'll be able to use in other businesses. Although I'm working in publishing at the moment, marketing is a part of every industry.

Periodical publishing

About 18,000 people in total are employed in publishing more than 5000 periodical titles in this country. These include weekly and monthly magazines, comics, business, trade and professional journals. Many of the jobs, as with book publishing, are in support services such as accountancy, transport, marketing and computing. The specialist areas are editorial work, the art desk, advertisement sales, and circulation.

Editorial work

The editorial staff of a magazine usually consists of a production editor, who is the link between the writing team and the printer, and a couple of sub-editors, who turn raw material into finished articles to appear in the magazine. The editorial staff also commission articles from freelance writers – relatively few periodicals employ staff journalists – and may themselves also research and write contributions, depending on the size of the magazine.

The way into editorial positions, especially on the more general publications such as women's magazines, is often through training and experience as a magazine journalist. However, highly specialist publications, such as medical journals, cookery and craft magazines and fine art publications, need editorial staff qualified in appropriate subjects, who have a complete understanding of the subject matter of the magazine and of their readers' needs.

The art desk

As in book publishing, there is a design team to decide on graphics and typography, to lay out the pages and illustrations, commission photographs and artists, and to deal with all other aspects of the visual appearance of the finished product.

Advertisement sales

Without income from advertisements to subsidise them, few periodicals could survive. Advertisement space is sold either direct to firms which have appropriate products to publicise, or through the advertising agency which they employ. Space sellers must be able to identify the people with the power to buy space, and be able to convince them through statistical information and a knowledge of the particular readership, that an advertisement would be worthwhile. These posts are for extroverts who can work on their own initiative, and advertisement sales can be a first step towards further work on a periodical.

Circulation

Circulation staff plan the production figures of the periodical, and its distribution to potential purchasers. Circulation figures are vital to the advertisement sales department and are usually audited independently to let potential advertisers judge fairly whether or not to buy space. Circulation staff promote subscription sales, maximise orders from the wholesale trade, calculate budget figures, forecast future sales, and plan the distribution of the magazines from the printers to the wholesalers.

GETTING STARTED IN PUBLISHING

Book publishing

At the editorial level, which is the most popular, book publishing is normally a career for graduates, though there are occasional openings for those with A levels. However, even with a degree, getting started is very difficult. There are specific degrees in publishing, but the degree subject is relatively unimportant unless you want to work in musical, educational or scientific publishing or other areas, where an appropriate degree can certainly help. Graduate training schemes are rare, so finding a post means producing a good CV, writing to firms and watching the press for suitable posts. Competition for both advertised and unadvertised positions for trainees is fierce. Starting in a secretarial post is one entry route which has proved successful for many sub-editors, and computer literacy is almost essential, as new technology is widespread.

Vacancies appear in various newspapers and periodicals. The *Writer's and Artist's Year Book* will tell you which publishers specialise in subjects where you have a particular interest or aptitude.

If you do get invited to an interview, make sure you are familiar with that particular publisher's catalogue, as well as with the industry as a whole. Getting the first job is the biggest hurdle – once you're in, chances of promotion are reasonably good.

Periodical publishing

Much the same advice applies as above, for book publishing, though journalistic experience is likely to be important for some types of work. Some large publishers run in-house training schemes for graduates.

SPECIALIST COURSES IN PUBLISHING

For these courses, other than degrees and BTEC HNDs, note that no mandatory awards are made by LEAs. Discretionary awards may be available from your local education authority, but few of these awards are made.

First degrees (honours) in publishing are offered at various universities. Two A levels/Advanced GNVQ/BTEC National Diploma are the normal minimum entry requirements.

Other courses include a BTEC HND/HNC in printing, publishing and packaging, and electronic publishing. Various universities offer postgraduate courses.

There are also courses in printing technology, production and management which include publishing and are useful for those wishing to enter the production management side of publishing.

Those interested in design should look at graphic design degrees or BTEC courses which include book or print design specialisms.

National Vocational Qualifications are available in publishing for people who already have experience in the industry. For further information, contact Book House Training Centre or the Open Learning Validation Services (see Further Information section).

Careers related to publishing

Bookselling can provide a useful introduction to the sales side of publishing. The Booksellers' Association has lists of firms, including those listed as chartered booksellers, who give training.

Copy editors and proof-readers often work on a **freelance** basis. The Society of Freelance Editors and Proof-readers gives information and advice, and offers training courses on basic skills, through to more advanced topics. These courses, however, carry no guarantee of work.

The Society's accreditation and registration scheme (launched in November 1995) provides a career-enhancement route for the more experienced freelance worker.

Indexers are usually employed on a freelance basis to prepare indexes. The Society of Indexers can provide information on training and finding work. Their correspondence course usually takes at least six months to complete.

Literary agents act as intermediaries between publishers and authors. Agents usually work for small firms or on their own. They have, in most cases, moved from publishing into agency work.

Picture researchers are often freelance, and provide a service to publishers on the acquisition of suitable pictures, their cost, and likely quality of reproduction. This is a very specialised area where sound knowledge of galleries, museums, specialist collections, etc, is needed.

For details of courses and entry requirements, consult reference books on higher education in your local school, college or careers centre library – works such as *University and College Entrance*, the CRAC Degree Course Guides, the *Compendium of Higher Education*, etc, or use the ECCTIS computer database.

DESKTOP PUBLISHING

> Desktop publishing is a by-product of the computer revolution and the great changes that have happened in printing. Desktop publishing work is used in printing, publishing and in many areas of industry and commerce. Effective DTP work requires an understanding of printing terminology, an eye for design and confidence with computers.

Until perhaps fifteen years ago, Caxton, the father of printing in the fifteenth century, could have entered a print works and understood what was going on. Now, almost every mechanical process, except the actual printing, has been replaced by electronics. All the editing, layout and preparation of books, magazines and newspapers can be done using computer keyboards and screens. There is also no reason why these processes have to be done by professional printers. As the power of personal computers has increased, it has become possible to run the very complicated programs needed for publishing on ordinary home or office computers. Now, authors can prepare books for printing (although, in practice, they usually don't) and local societies can produce their own newsletters to a high standard.

The term *desktop publishing*, or DTP for short, is a rather vague term for a lot of different processes. DTP equipment and techniques can be used to produce anything from a small, photocopied newsletter to the finished artwork of an expensive book. There are various DTP programs, aimed at both professional

and amateur users, and, although the basic ideas are similar, the techniques can be very different. This also means that the wide range of employers who use DTP need very different levels of skill from the DTP operators or designers. DTP users can be highly trained graphic designers, office typists who have learned limited skills, or individuals who have taught themselves the techniques for a particular purpose.

DTP in printing

Origination in printing is now largely electronic. Much of the text for printed material arrives in the form of wordprocessed documents, which the printer prepares for final printing.

Decisions about what typeface, layout and colours to use can be made at a keyboard and then transmitted directly to the photographic process used in making the printing plates.

General DTP work

Because DTP is comparatively cheap and simple to operate, many firms and organisations are using it to produce general office publications such as forms and information leaflets, and even advertising and publicity materials. DTP skills are likely to be combined with other skills, including wordprocessing and possibly other computer work.

TRAINING

You can look for training with a printing firm where you could become a typesetter.

There are also short courses in DTP, run at colleges of further education, where you can get a basic grounding in DTP techniques. To get the full benefit from a short course, you do need to have access to a computer to practise on and develop your skills. DTP programs are a great deal more complicated than wordprocessing, and take some time to master properly.

RSA Examinations Board offers qualifications in Desktop Publishing. Contact RSA's Customer Information Bureau on 01203 470033 for further details. If you want private training, contact suppliers of DTP programs.

PRESS PHOTOGRAPHER

> **Press photographers** add to the visual appeal of newspapers through the use of photographs – recording events and news stories with their cameras. Those working for national newspapers may specialise – in sports photography, for example. **Photojournalists** usually work for magazines rather than newspapers and provide the words for a story as well as the pictures.

Photographers can work as employees on the staff of a paper or a magazine, or on a freelance basis – offering their pictures to any paper or magazine which might be interested. Freelance photographers often sell their work to small magazines and local papers and periodicals. If they're very lucky, freelancers occasionally get a scoop of an unexpected newsworthy happening which they can sell to one of the national papers. The work of the press photographer can include both routine and highly exciting elements. Much can depend on the type of paper or magazine for which you work.

Working for a national daily or an international bureau, press photographers are often under considerable pressure. Conditions in which they are required to take pictures are often very crowded and uncomfortable and, sometimes, extremely dangerous – think of war reports, for instance. Photographic scoops are of considerable importance to a newspaper's sales, and editors always expect their photographers to get the best and most daring shots.

Starting a career

The ways into freelance photography can be many and varied, and a career may develop from a broader photographic training or even from a hobby. Freelance photographers very often have another occupation which provides their basic means of living, with their income from photography as a bonus. It is not possible to generalise about training for freelance work other than to state the obvious – that you will need to be as skilful a photographer as possible, with equipment and knowledge to produce results which equal those of professional photographers. With experience, it is possible for freelancers to become members of the National Union of Journalists or Institute of Journalists.

TRAINING

There are two main training routes into press photography.

Direct entry
You can apply directly to an editor for an indentured traineeship under the national scheme of the National Council for the Training of Journalists (NCTJ). Five GCSEs at grade C, including English, or possibly an Intermediate GNVQ, are required. Press photographers receive the same basic rates of pay as other journalists, and trainee photographers serve similar indentures to those of trainee reporters, attending eight-week courses at Sheffield College in their first and second years and working towards a National Certificate.

Pre-entry course
The National Council for the Training of Journalists runs a one-year full-time pre-entry course in press photography. Applications for the course must be made directly to the NCTJ. You would normally need a minimum of five GCSEs at grade C (with one subject also at A level) including English language, or qualifications of equivalent standard. This would be followed by a period of on-the-job training with a newspaper. The annual intake for the course is very small and competition for places is fierce. Grants for the course are discretionary, so check with your local education authority whether an award can be made.

Adults: applicants over 30 years of age may have individual training arrangements agreed with the employing editor, but would still be expected to achieve the standards required of indentured trainees.

just THE JOB

WORK WITH LANGUAGES

There are many jobs which require the ability to speak and write one or more foreign languages, apart from the very specific tasks of translators and interpreters. Some jobs can be done with a reasonable conversational ability, while others demand fluency in a complicated legal or technical vocabulary. Opportunities range from those requiring good GCSEs to degree-level and professional qualifications.

Britons have a poor reputation when it comes to speaking foreign languages. As tourists, and even in business, we have always relied on the fact that people from other countries are willing to learn English! But this attitude needs to change. Many British companies are trading in and with European countries, and European companies have more bases here in Britain. We are at a disadvantage if we can't conduct business in the languages of the countries in which we want to sell our products or market our services.

Better job opportunities!

With job qualifications becoming more acceptable throughout the European Union, people of one country will be able to carry out their job or profession in any other country. This won't just apply to people working in things like the law, accountancy, engineering, teaching and so on; it will be just the same for jobs requiring fewer qualifications – garage and factory work, nursing and hospital services, shop work, building, etc.

So, if you want to try for jobs abroad, which may well pay a lot more than in Britain, you need to speak other languages.

This is all quite different from the days when a job with languages meant translating and interpreting, or teaching a language. And it's not just in contacts with European countries that language abilities are needed. There is a serious lack of people able to communicate in languages such as Russian, Japanese, Chinese and Arabic.

As a general rule, language skills need to be accompanied by other skills or specialised knowledge – such as secretarial skills, information or librarianship skills, journalistic skills and a wide range of other professional and technical qualifications. Providing you have these other skills – and the right sort of personality and other aptitudes to suit particular types of work – there are many areas of work in which languages can be a real asset.

So the need for people with ability in languages is increasing. Without them, we will be at a huge disadvantage in competing for jobs, in carrying out business conversations, understanding reports and selling our products.

What about jobs for linguists as such?

There aren't so many jobs where the main ability needed is that of speaking or writing a language fluently. Even where languages play a major role in a career, it is helpful to have other experience as well.

Interpreters and translators

The demand for interpreters and translators is steady, but the numbers required are not great. There are about 200 agencies in London which deal with translating and interpreting; many of those employed by the agencies are freelance rather than salaried. The jobs which exist normally go to people fluent in two or more languages – often translators and interpreters have been bilingual or trilingual from birth. The biggest employer of interpreters is the European Commission, which requires knowledge of at least two other community languages besides English. The United Nations has similar requirements. (See next section.)

Teaching

In schools, colleges, higher education or specialist language colleges, teaching is the most obvious and most likely way of really using your languages. There is a shortage of language teachers at present and for the foreseeable future. The Teacher Training Agency has been given funds to help teacher training providers recruit candidates onto one-year and two-year secondary courses for priority subjects such as foreign languages.

Good language teachers need the right personality, besides their ability in languages. They must be excellent communicators, be able to motivate pupils and students, and they should have the resourcefulness to work out successful techniques for teaching language – e.g. through role-play, drama, etc. (See the book on *Teaching* in the *Just the Job!* series.)

Jobs with scope for using languages

Here are some ideas of jobs which offer particular opportunities for using languages. They certainly aren't the *only* ones – as mentioned earlier, opportunities in almost all types of work can be enhanced if you can communicate in a suitable foreign language.

Bilingual/trilingual secretarial work

There is a steady demand for good secretaries with a knowledge of foreign languages. International bodies and organisations with export and overseas departments provide opportunities. Specialist secretarial/linguist courses are available. The best job opportunities are likely to go to those who have taken such a course after foreign language A levels, or a foreign language degree.

Civil Service

There are some departments requiring a knowledge of foreign languages, such as Government Communication Headquarters and the Immigration Service. In the Diplomatic Service, an aptitude for languages is certainly an asset, but, as the languages required are often not taught in school, training would be given on-the-job. The more specialist jobs are for language graduates, but there are administrative posts which have lower entry requirements.

Librarianship and information science

Industrial and other specialist libraries, as well as public and university libraries, maintain collections of foreign books and journals. Librarians and information specialists may need to use materials produced in other languages in the course of their work. There are first degrees in library and/or information science/management which include language studies.

Travel and tourism

The tourist industry offers opportunities in this country and abroad. Areas in which languages are needed include working as cabin crew on aeroplanes, hovercraft, ships, etc; ground jobs in airports; working as a resort representative for British holidaymakers abroad; checking out holiday facilities as a tour operator; acting as a guide or courier to foreign visitors to Britain. The holiday season has become more prolonged, with autumn and winter breaks now commonplace. However, many guides and couriers work on a seasonal basis and full-time career opportunities in that area may be limited.

There are opportunities in travel and tourism to use all kinds of foreign languages, though the more common European ones (French, German, Spanish and Italian) may give the most scope overall. Business studies courses with an option in tourism exist for those aiming at management posts in the industry – and include study of foreign languages beyond A level.

Hotel and catering

An aptitude for foreign languages is useful to anyone looking for a job in catering, hotel management and hotel reception work, with the need to communicate with foreign visitors in their own language. There's also a lot of scope for workers at all levels to widen their experience by working abroad. A variety of courses exist for training at various levels and for different occupations.

Journalism

This is another area where language skills can be very useful, especially for the journalist working abroad.

Fine art and antiques

Dealing in top quality fine art and antiques is an international business, and there is a strong preference for people with language skills.

Law, insurance and finance

Membership of the European Union and the expansion of international trade have opened up new specialisms for accountants, lawyers, insurance professionals and other financial specialists. International law and finance is a complex area and there are highly paid jobs for those who specialise in it. Courses combining law and languages, or accountancy and languages, are offered at universities. For more information, consult prospectuses.

Sales, marketing and distribution

To survive as a trading nation we must export, so, increasingly, competence in languages is seen as important in industry and commerce. The whole area of marketing offers scope for language use because of the contacts with overseas trade, and this sort of work takes in graduate engineers, scientists and other personnel with technical skills, as well as non-technical people. There are business studies courses at various levels of entry, which offer language studies as a major part of the course, and degree courses in engineering and related subjects which include the study of foreign languages.

Which language?

European languages are widely taught to GCSE and A level in schools and colleges, with French being by far the most commonly available language. You may also get the chance to learn German, Spanish or Italian. These days, there is more emphasis in GCSE on 'getting by' in a language – the sort of things you need for everyday life.

It is worth considering that many people learn French, German and Spanish to quite a high standard. You will find that a less common, or less commonly taught, language can be equally valuable – or more so, because of its rarity value. Think about following a course in another European language, such as Italian, Dutch, Swedish or Greek, or in Russian, Japanese, a Middle Eastern or Indian language.

Languages can be learned through short courses or evening classes, available in many colleges of further education and through independent language schools. Open learning packages with audio-tapes are also available. Such courses could lead to GCSE, A level or Institute of Linguists exams. The Institute of Linguists provide examinations in over thirty languages.

HIGHER EDUCATION
Degree courses
The serious linguist would be looking towards a degree course at a university or college of higher education. These generally last four years, with one year being spent abroad to let you improve your language skills – as an assistant in a school, by working in an industrial or commercial firm, or attending a foreign university.

There are also many joint degrees lasting three or four years, where you can study a language plus another major subject; the second subject could be almost anything – business studies, English, history, information studies, law, science, etc.

You can start many languages from scratch at universities and colleges. For instance, Spanish and German can be taken from scratch and, of course, all the less usual languages are offered on this basis.

Postgraduate courses
There is quite a variety of courses available to the graduate, including teacher training, courses for bilingual secretaries/personal assistants, diplomas in translating and interpreting, masters' degrees in information studies, bilingual masters' degrees in business administration and many others.

Some advertisements for jobs requiring language skills

Information officer – *'An international organisation urgently requires an information officer to work in its business information, membership and services department. The successful candidate is expected to have a university degree and at least three years' experience in translation work from Arabic to English and English to Arabic. Postgraduate qualifications will be an advantage. Experience in research and compiling information on trade and business matters between the UK and Arab states is essential.'*

Export sales engineer – *'A leading manufacturer of electric vehicle controllers requires a highly capable German-speaking sales engineer to develop business in Germany. A technical background in electrical/electronic engineering is highly desirable. Regular UK and overseas travel is envisaged and the job is both responsible and demanding.'*

Market researcher/report writer – *'An international organisation in London urgently requires a bilingual report writer and market researcher to work in its market research department. The successful candidate is expected to be fluent in written and spoken English and Japanese with at least two years' translation experience. They should be able to research and write reports of a detailed technical nature in both languages. A business school diploma and experience of marketing between the UK and Japan is essential. A willingness to travel and a driver's licence are required.'*

Editorial assistant – *'Graduate in Italian studies required as secretarial/editorial assistant in the London office of an Italian publisher.'*

TRANSLATING & INTERPRETING

> When people think of jobs using languages, translating and interpreting are often the two that come to mind. It may come as a surprise to discover that only a tiny percentage of language graduates actually go into these areas of work. You have to be very good at your chosen language(s) to be able to make a living at either translating or interpreting.

Your first step on the long trail to getting this kind of work will probably be to get a degree. The question is, *which* language to study? At school you will have had the opportunity to study French, German and possibly Spanish and Russian. If you seriously intend to be a linguist, you will probably be taking two languages at A level. You can either continue in higher education with the languages you are already studying, or start learning a completely new language. The British higher education system offers degrees in all major and many minor world languages, so the choice is wide, and the question is which ones are going to be most useful. Since most translating and interpreting work is concerned with commercial and technical communications, the key languages are Arabic, Chinese (Cantonese and Mandarin), Dutch, English, French, German, Japanese, Portuguese, Russian, Spanish, Swedish and the eastern European languages.

Courses which combine a language with a technological or commercial subject are particularly useful, as most translators specialise. There are some postgraduate courses in translating and interpreting skills, and some short courses for non-graduates.

Translator

Only small numbers of people are involved in translating and most of them work on short, technical and business texts of various types. There are very few people engaged on the translation of full-length plays and books. Most are freelance and work part-time. All kinds of writings need to be translated, such as textbooks, scripts and travel guides. Literary translators of major works are often well-known authors or academics. At the very least, a good knowledge of the source language and its literature is required, together with an ability to write well in your own language. The Translators Association provides advice and services to translators of full-length works.

Technical translators usually work freelance for a translation agency, often working from home. As well as fluency in at least one language, a knowledge of the specialised vocabulary used in, say, engineering, medicine or pharmaceuticals is necessary. The Institute of Translating and Interpreting provides an employment and contact service for translators and interpreters who meet their stringent entrance requirements. Some large firms also employ their own translators, where large amounts of work need to be done routinely. Even in the largest firms, translation only provides work for a few people. Bear in mind that translators should work only into their home language and not translate into a foreign language. The Institute of Linguists also keeps registers of its translator and interpreter members for prospective employers.

The BBC monitoring service at Caversham employs translators who listen to overseas broadcasts and provide transcriptions for government and news agency purposes. Many countries' broadcasts are monitored, so a wide range of language specialists are needed. The Civil Service employs translators at the Government Communications HQ in Cheltenham, with occasional vacancies in other departments such as defence, trade and industry, and food and fisheries. In general, the diplomatic service is interested in those with a flair for languages, but not particularly in specialist translators.

Computer translating systems leave a lot to be desired, so are unlikely to take over people's jobs yet. However, computerised dictionaries and glossaries, wordprocessing systems and fax machines are widely used. Freelance translators will need to buy some expensive equipment.

Interpreter

Interpreters differ from translators in that they provide spoken translations rather than written ones. They are a very select band indeed, and recruitment is severely limited.

Interpreters work at high-level international meetings, translating speeches into English (interpreters usually work from the foreign language into their home language). Interpretation is either *simultaneous*, where the speaker's words are passed on as the speech is being delivered, or *consecutive*, where the speech is summarised and translated later. The simultaneous method is more commonly used nowadays.

Conference interpreters work at the United Nations, the EC and other international assemblies, and on a freelance basis at international conferences. Interpreters at meetings between individuals have to work equally well in both languages. This is called *liaison* or *bilingual* interpreting. Interpreters for courts, airlines and industrial concerns are usually drawn from employees or known linguists, and called upon when needed.

Permanent posts for interpreters are rare. The European

Commission is the world's largest employer of interpreters, all of whom need to know at least two of the community languages besides English. It recruits graduates for a six-month training course in conference interpreting. Other employers include the United Nations, NATO, the International Atomic Energy Authority and various bodies such as international trade organisations. Like translators, many interpreters work on a freelance basis, getting their work through agencies. Most need some other work that they can do between interpreting jobs, and they often undertake translation work.

Interpreting is very demanding, requiring quick wits, fast reactions, strong nerves and good health. It is rather like taking a continuous oral examination. Rates of pay are excellent and much of the work takes place in glamorous and prestigious surroundings.

Adults: as years of experience in using a language are necessary for interpreters and translators, this is a career where maturity and experience can be an advantage. Freelance part-time translating work can fit in well with domestic commitments, but interpreting can involve travelling – often at short notice.

just THE JOB

WORKING IN THE MEDIA

> Work in the media is concerned with the channels through which information and entertainment is transmitted to the public, such as newspapers, magazines, videos and films, radio or television. You may be providing materials and information like photographs, film sequences or written copy, or working on the design side. Alternatively, you could be employed in an area which *uses* the media, like advertising or public relations.

Media work has a glamorous image and the competition to get started is always tough. The more training and experience you can get before you start applying for jobs, the better. There is a wide range of specialised courses in subjects like journalism and graphic design, and also courses in media studies, which give a general introduction to the media world.

Journalism

The main areas of employment for journalists are the local press, the national press, news agencies, the vast range of periodicals published weekly and monthly and, of course, radio and television. The main employer of new entrants is the provincial press. Here, trainee journalists can learn the basic skills under less pressure than on the national papers. There is little chance of moving into the national press until you have three years' experience as a qualified journalist on a provincial paper. (See earlier section.)

Radio and television

This is the most glamorous and high-profile area of media work. But, as with icebergs, the public only see the top end! For every successful TV personality or star, there are hundreds of technicians, journalists, PAs, researchers, studio managers and designers working away in the background, many of whom do not even get a mention in the credits at the end of a programme. Unfortunately, there are only a very few starter jobs for people without experience, so determination and persistence are needed in order to get a job.

Design

Design is communicating through visual means, which could be print, drawings, photographs or combinations of all three. Media work can include book illustration (which is almost fine art), advertising and packaging, technical illustration and typography. The scope for design work has increased tremendously with the development of advertising, the expansion of the media and a growing awareness throughout industry of the importance of company image and style.

Photography

There is a lot of work in the media for photographers. As well as opportunities for press photographers and photojournalists (see earlier section), there is a tremendous amount of high quality photography needed in advertising, magazine features and publicity. Photographers usually do a college course before starting a job.

Film and video

The film industry does not recruit a large number of new entrants, so it is difficult to find openings. Television companies have a higher staff turnover, however, and initial opportunities (particularly in the technical areas) can arise in this area. The production of videos for a wide range of applications other than

broadcasting is a rapidly expanding field. Videos are used for training purposes, teaching, publicity, sales campaigns, advertising and public relations.

Publishing

Publishing is a highly competitive business where sound editorial skills, commercial judgement, marketing and advertising skills are vital for survival. Most book publishers make their profits from educational, technical and scientific books; others specialise in either fiction or non-fiction for the general public. At the editorial level, which is the most popular work area, book publishing is a career for graduates, although there can be very occasional openings for those with A levels. (See earlier section.)

Advertising

Advertising is a young, often glamorous, tough and highly competitive business. Advertising needs designers and photographers to supply the pictures, and copywriters to provide the words. Scriptwriters and production crews work on TV, radio and cinema advertisements, whilst media planners and space buyers make sure that, once made, the advertisement is seen. (See later section.)

EDUCATION AND TRAINING FOR THE MEDIA

It is not easy to generalise about education and training in an area of work where there is so much variety. For further information, look for the relevant section in this book or other title in the *Just the Job!* series. In many areas of work there is no need to take a specialised course, even at degree level. Competition for places on media courses is intense, but by no means everyone working in the media has a degree in media studies. A very high proportion do, however, have degrees, for example in politics, history, engineering or science. It is also worth remembering that, for many jobs, you can only train once you are in. You may well need to take any starter job you can, and then change direction. The BBC has a particularly good internal staff training scheme.

//just THE JOB

BROADCASTING – PRODUCTION & PRESENTATION

The broadcasting industry is big business and employs a lot of people, many in the field of information. In trying to get into this sort of work, you will be taking on quite a challenge and competing with a lot of bright and ambitious people. As the industry becomes more competitive and cost-conscious, jobs are less likely to be full-time or permanent.

Research assistant

Careful research must be carried out before a programme can be made. **Researchers** are employed, usually on contract, for a programme or series. They are usually bright young graduates looking for a way into television; researchers can gain useful experience working as the most junior member of a production team. While they are often recruited internally from staff with broadcasting experience, the most useful experience outside television itself would be in journalism. Getting the first job can be very difficult. Very occasionally broadcasting companies advertise for **trainee researchers**, but these adverts attract thousands of replies. A possible course of action is to approach producers and directors yourself. A booklet called *Contacts,* produced by *Spotlight* magazine, lists all the senior production staff in TV and radio.

Presenter

Presenters can be actors, newsreaders, journalists, experts on particular subjects or just personalities, such as famous sportsmen or women. There are no formal routes into this sort of job and every presenter's experience is slightly different. Most presenters have a proven track record, whether through local radio experience in interviewing and reporting, or perhaps through winning Wimbledon! Whatever the background, it is essential to have a suitable broadcasting voice. A journalistic background is certainly highly recommended, and further training is given, where necessary, by the employer. Presenters are usually employed on fixed-term contracts.

Where are the jobs?
Local radio

The network of local radio stations, BBC and others, covers the entire country. The output of commercial stations is dominated by local news and pop music, and you will need an interest in these areas of work to get started on Capital FM, Severn Sound or wherever. BBC local radio tends to have more talk and less music. Many people begin their careers in local radio stations. Local radio producers tend to be Jacks and Jills of all trades.

National radio

Classic FM, Virgin Radio, TALK Radio UK, Independent Radio News, Network News, Atlantic 252, and the five major BBC radio stations are all heard nationwide. Specialist producers work in light entertainment, sport, drama, news and current affairs, music and features. Some may start with a background in local radio; others begin as production trainees, or move in from other jobs in broadcasting. Drama and light entertainment producers may have theatre experience and music producers may be trained musicians. The bulk of jobs are in London, but BBC regional centres offer some opportunities, mainly in Bristol, Cardiff, Manchester, Birmingham and Glasgow.

BBC World Service

This internationally respected service is run from Bush House in London. Programmes are mainly concerned with news and current affairs. Linguists with a keen interest in broadcasting can sometimes get started here, though most language services are staffed by nationals of the target country of the transmissions.

BBC TV

The biggest single employer of producers and directors, again mainly in London, but in the regions as well. Production staff are usually employed on contracts, rather than salaried.

ITV

The regional structure of ITV means that jobs are scattered round the country. (A list of companies is given in the Further Information section.) The smaller companies originate very little of their own material and therefore have less need of production/direction staff.

Independent contractors

A growing sector of the industry, with companies varying in size from half a dozen personnel, to large organisations on the scale of Carlton. Many programmes you see now are produced by these independent production companies. The production staff of one of these companies will develop an idea, and sell it to Channel 4 or one of the other networks, who will then recruit a contract crew and director to make the programme. Opportunities in this area are usually confined to experienced operators – finance will not run to trainees.

Satellite broadcasting companies offer similar jobs. The major one in the UK is British Sky Broadcasting, or BSkyB. There are also limited opportunities with cable television companies, although they do not offer the wide range of programming that the major terrestrial and satellite broadcasters do.

ADVERTISING

Advertising involves several different careers, all based around promoting products or services. It is a young, tough and highly competitive business which is often seen as glamorous. Many of the top jobs go to graduates, but there are opportunities for people with lower qualifications. Keenness and creativity are all-important.

Advertising agencies

Agencies are employed by manufacturing and retail companies, service industries, charities, government departments and political parties to produce advertisements. They advise on the best media to use (posters, radio, TV, newspapers, magazines), and place advertisements appropriately. Agencies must produce work quickly and under pressure, yet pay meticulous attention to detail and accuracy. **Account executives** oversee and take responsibility for the work of one client, account or campaign. **Account planners** work with account executives, and their function is to understand what is happening in the market place and to represent the consumer on the account team.

Other members of the account team include designers, photographers, art directors and copywriters to supply the creative work. Scriptwriters and production crews work on TV, radio and cinema adverts, and media planners and buyers of advertising space make sure that, once made, the advertisement is seen. There are also staff responsible for marketing and research, print and mechanical production, and control of finance. Many of the staff in these jobs are likely to have been trained in a particular aspect, such as graphic art or accountancy, before joining the advertising business. The majority of people employed in advertising are not in the most creative and glamorous jobs, but provide the essential support and back-up for the designers and writers.

Jobs as account executives, planners and copywriters are highly sought after and, in most cases, go to bright, ambitious graduates. If you are not a graduate, you might try and get a start in some fairly routine job, or as a secretary, and hope to make people notice your creativity and drive that way. Most advertising agencies are small, and numbers overall in the agency business are few. The London area offers the most jobs, but there are also agencies in cities and even in small towns.

Tasneem – junior advertising account executive in a London-based agency

'It was very difficult to get a job in advertising. This was the fifth job in this type of work that I had been interviewed for. Now I'm here, I wonder what I have let myself in for! As a graduate trainee (I spent three years getting a degree in business studies), I work for a short time in each department so I can learn as I go.

I have been helping to plan advertising campaigns, and have just been given my own account for the first time. Although I will still be supervised, I am the one who has to interview the clients to work out exactly what they want, and to find out everything I can about them and their products. I then have to explain this to the creative team (the art director and copywriter) so that they can create the words and the visuals. It's quite a responsibility, and I am feeling nervous – but confident that I can do a

> *good job. The hardest bit will be to get everything done in time so that I can present it to the clients on schedule. No doubt this will mean a few more late nights!*
>
> *Although I like working here, if I want promotion, I will have to consider moving to another agency.*

Advertising media

Advertising messages can be transmitted to their intended target in various ways – newspapers, magazines, outdoor hoardings, posters, radio, television, cinema and direct mailing are all possibilities. These are called the **advertising media**. Staff in the various media sell advertising space. Their job is to persuade customers that their particular form of communication is the most effective. They arrange the publication or transmission of material sent in by agencies and the advertising departments of firms and businesses. **Media sales** is a very high-pressure job, in which numeracy and personality are very important.

Advertising and publicity departments

Most large firms and organisations have an advertising and publicity department. Here, staff coordinate all the different aspects of promoting an image of the organisation and its products. They decide, for instance, when it is appropriate to employ the services of advertising agencies, when to organise trade exhibitions and fairs, when to make direct mailshots. A job in such a department could be a useful start to a wider career in advertising, or could provide a career in itself.

Advertising services

There are various trades and businesses providing services to advertising. These offer career opportunities in their own right, but might also provide a background for work in an agency, after training and experience. Much advertising involves print work, so experience in aspects of printing, dealing with packaging and graphics in particular, could be relevant to advertising. Knowledge of plate-making, typesetting and other methods of producing images for magazines and newspapers, are also transferable skills. Trained graphic artists may move from design studios into advertising agencies. Experience and training in photography could be a starting point for a career in the creative or design side of advertising, and people with skills and experience in radio, film and television often move into the business of making commercials.

EDUCATION AND TRAINING

There are some full-time courses specifically designed to equip you for work in advertising, such as BTEC Higher National Diplomas in advertising design or copywriting, or BA(Hons) degrees in the areas of advertising media and media management, design and marketing. These courses are offered mainly by the new universities. Many colleges offer diploma courses in advertising design or copywriting.

Generally, if you are aiming for account executive, planner or copywriting jobs, it will help to be a graduate – any subject can be acceptable. If you are not a graduate, you should certainly have a good general education. Look out for business and finance courses, and subjects such as communications and media studies. Most art directors and designers have at least a BTEC Higher National qualification in graphic design.

You could apply to take the professional exams of CAM (Communication, Advertising and Marketing Education Foundation), who offer nationally recognised certificate and diploma courses in advertising. However, a professional qualification is not essential for entry to an advertising agency. Write to CAM for details.

PUBLIC RELATIONS

> Public relations work covers all the aspects of establishing good relations between an organisation and its public, whether that means customers, shareholders or a surrounding community. Most public relations executives are graduates, but there are other jobs in the industry which do not require such high qualifications.

Local and national government, nationalised and private industry, professional bodies and charities all rely on good public relations. They must present a good public image of their organisation – and not neglect letting their own staff know what is going on. Maintaining goodwill and mutual understanding is a delicate business: the balance is always shifting, so this is a job which requires careful forward planning and sustained effort.

Public relations, as an industry, has grown enormously in recent decades. It is closely related both to journalism and to advertising. Much of the work involves writing material, or using the media in such a way that the organisation involved is presented in a good light. **Public relations officers** may write press releases, arrange TV or radio interviews, organise exhibitions and produce magazines or pamphlets. They attend meetings and discussions with clients and employers, and research the background to a particular public relations problem, perhaps to provide material for a company manager's speech at a function.

Working situations vary a lot. Some public relations officers

work for one firm; others work for a public relations consultancy firm with many different clients.

What it takes

A good public relations officer or consultant needs to be the type of person who can:

- think ahead;
- react quickly to new situations;
- get on well with a wide range of people;

- put across a point of view firmly without being annoying;
- be flexible in their outlook as the needs of their clients vary.

A thick skin is necessary too, as the public relations officer is the person who has to deal with the indignant customer and the probing journalist.

QUALIFICATIONS AND TRAINING

There is no set pattern of training for public relations, although, in practice, most public relations officers have degrees. Any degree subject is likely to be acceptable. Many move into the work from journalism, the media or advertising. Some entrants start on a firm's general management training scheme and then specialise in public relations work. The larger consultancies recruit a few graduates direct from higher education.

There are first degree, Higher National Diploma and postgraduate courses either in public relations, or including an element of public relations in business subjects, at a number of universities and colleges. There are several degree courses in communications and media studies which could be useful, as well as one-year pre-journalism courses available at various colleges. Once employed in public relations, there are courses leading to the qualifications of the Communication, Advertising and Marketing Education Foundation (CAM). Holders of the CAM Diploma (or of other, approved, academic qualifications) can become members of the Institute of Public Relations.

It is also possible to start on the clerical or secretarial side of a public relations firm or department, with the aim of moving into the professional work after gaining a general background. Public relations firms usually demand a high level of secretarial skills. Typing and wordprocessing qualifications are very useful for anyone hoping to work in public relations.

POLITICS

There are many jobs involved with politics – being a Member of Parliament or local councillor; a senior civil servant; a constituency worker. Many of the jobs involve information and research work. For many posts you need academic qualifications, in some cases to degree level, and perhaps a commitment to a particular political party; for others you need an interest in the community.

Party headquarters staff

The major parties all employ staff in their regional and national headquarters' offices. They work on collecting and giving information, writing speeches, working with party committees, organising public relations in general, and keeping the media up to date with party activities. They may also be involved with research work. Here, a good education is essential, and most research workers have degrees in subjects such as economics or politics. Again, involvement with voluntary party work and student or youth politics is important.

Some people are also employed by the major parties in Europe.

Parliamentary jobs

Some Members of Parliament and peers have **secretarial** and **research** staff. Individuals are responsible for recruiting their own staff. Secretarial skills and experience and interest in politics are important for these jobs. Researchers are likely to be graduates.

Civil Service and local government work

Although strictly non-political in terms of favouring one party or another, many higher-level Civil Service and local government posts involve working with politicians and dealing with matters which are basically political. The political masters rely on government servants to provide them with the information on which they base decisions, and to do the background organising which keeps both national and local government working. The European Commission offers similar opportunities.

Journalism

Journalists are often involved in politics, either reporting for the media or working in a press office of a particular party. Television, radio, newspapers and periodicals all employ political journalists. The job of **political correspondent** on a newspaper would only go to a very experienced journalist with a good deal of basic experience, as well as a highly developed interest in the subject. Obviously, you would first need to train as a journalist (see earlier section on journalism).

FOR FURTHER INFORMATION

WRITING FOR A LIVING
Society of Authors – 84 Drayton Gardens, London SW10 9SB. Tel: 0171 373 6642.
Society of Indexers – 38 Rochester Road, London NW1 9JJ. Tel: 0171 916 7809.
Writer's Guild of Great Britain – 430 Edgware Road, London W2 1EH. Tel: 0171 723 8074.

Writer's and Artist's Year Book, published by A & C Black – can be consulted in your local public library.

JOURNALISM
Chartered Institute of Journalists – 2 Dock Offices, Surrey Quays Road, London SE16 2XL. Tel: 0171 252 1187.
National Council for the Training of Broadcast Journalists – Council Secretary, 188 Lichfield Court, Sheen Road, Richmond, Surrey TW9 1BB. Tel: 0181 940 0694.
National Council for the Training of Journalists – Latton Bush Centre, Southern Way, Harlow, Essex CM18 7BL. Tel: 01279 430009 – for information on courses.
National Union of Journalists – Acorn House, 314–320 Gray's Inn Road, London WC1X 8DP. Tel: 0171 278 7916.
The Newspaper Society – Training Department, Bloomsbury House, Bloomsbury Square, 74–77 Great Russell Street, London WC1B 3DA. Tel: 0171 636 7014.
Periodical Publishers' Association Ltd – Imperial House, 15–19 Kingsway, London WC2B 6UN. Tel: 0171 379 6268.
Periodicals Training Council – address as for the Periodical Publishers' Association. Tel: 0171 836 8798.

Working in Journalism, published by COIC.

Careers in Journalism, published by Kogan Page.
Journalism and Authorship, an AGCAS careers information leaflet for graduates, available from Central Services Unit, Crawford House, Precinct Centre, Manchester M13 9EP. Tel: 0161 273 4233.

LIBRARY AND INFORMATION WORK
ASLIB (The Association for Information Management) – 20-24 Old Street, London EC1V 9AP. Tel: 0171 253 4488.
Institute of Information Scientists – 44–45 Museum Street, London WC1A 1LY. Tel: 0171 831 8003.
Institute of Scientific and Technical Communicators – Kings Court, 2–16 Goodge Street, London W1P 1FF. Tel: 0171 436 4425. Can provide information on courses.
The Library Association – Information Services, 7 Ridgmount Street, London WC1E 7AE. Tel: 0171 636 7543 – publishes free careers information.

ARCHIVE WORK
Society of Archivists – Information House, 20-24 Old Street, London EC1V 9AP. Tel: 0171 253 5087.

Heritage Management and Museum Work – an AGCAS graduate careers information booklet available from Central Services Unit, Crawford House, Precinct Centre, Manchester M13 9EP.
Archives as a Career is available from the Society of Archivists.
Record Repositories in Great Britain, published by HMSO, gives addresses of record offices and is available in reference libraries. You could also contact your local authority records office.

PUBLISHING AND DESKTOP PUBLISHING
Adobe Systems UK Ltd – Waterview House, 1 Roundwood Avenue, Stockley Park, Uxbridge, Middlesex UB11 9AE. Tel: 0181 453 2211 – for authorised trainers on PageMaker.
Book House Training Centre – 45 East Hill, London SW18 2QZ. Tel: 0181 874 2718/4608.
Open University Validation Services – 344–354 Gray's Inn Road, London WC1X 8BP.

Periodical Publishers' Association – Imperial House, 15–19 Kingsway, London WC2B 6UN. Tel: 0171 379 6268.
Publishers' Association – 19 Bedford Square, London WC1B 3HJ. Tel: 0171 580 6321.
Society of Freelance Editors and Proofreaders – 38 Rochester Road, London NW1 9JJ. Tel:0171 813 3113.
Women in Publishing and **The Society of Young Publishers** – c/o 12 Dyott Street, London WC1A 1DF.

Working in Publishing, published by COIC.
Careers in Publishing and Bookselling, published by Kogan Page.
Publishing Business, an AGCAS careers information leaflets for graduates, available from Central Services Unit, Crawford House, Precinct Centre, Manchester M13 9EP. Tel: 0161 273 4233.

WORK WITH LANGUAGES
Association for Language Learning – 150 Railway Terrace, Rugby CV21 3HN. Tel:01788 546443.
Centre for Information on Language Teaching and Research (CILT) – 20 Bedfordbury, London WC2N 4LB. Tel: 0171 379 5101.
Institute of Linguists – Mangold House, 24a Highbury Grove, London N5 2DQ. Tel: 0171 359 7445.
Institute of Translation and Interpreting – 377 City Road, London EC1V 1NA. Tel: 0171 713 7600.
The Translators Association – 84 Drayton Gardens, London SW10 9SB. Tel: 0171 373 6642.

The *Directory of Jobs and Careers Abroad* and the *Directory of Summer Jobs Abroad* are both published by Vacation Work, and may be available for reference in your careers service library, and school and college libraries.
Working in Languages, published by COIC.
Languages and Your Career, published by the Institute of Linguists.
Working Abroad, published by Kogan Page.
Careers using Languages, published by Kogan Page.

Using Languages, a graduate careers information leaflet, can be purchased from Central Services Unit, Crawford House, Precinct Centre, Oxford Road, Manchester M13 9EP.
So you think you'd like to be a translator or interpreter, published by the Institute of Translation and Interpreting.
Quick Guide to Literary Translation, available from The Translators Association.

WORKING IN THE MEDIA

Association of Independent Radio Companies Ltd – Radio House, 46 Westbourne Grove, London W2 5SH. Tel: 0171 727 2646.

BBC Recruitment Services – PO Box 7000, London W12 7ZY.

FT2 (Film Television Freelance Training) – 4th Floor, 5 Dean Street, London W1V 5RN. Tel: 0171 734 5141.

ITV Network Centre – 200 Gray's Inn Road, London WC1 8HF. Tel: 0171 843 8000.

Skillset – 124 Horseferry Road, London SW1P 2TX. Tel: 0171 306 8585.

Spotlight – 7 Leicester Place, London WC2H 7BP. Tel: 0171 437 7631.

Careers in Television and Radio, published by Kogan Page.
The *BBC* and *ITV Yearbooks*.
Education & Training for Film, Television and Broadcasting, published by BKSTS – The Moving Image Society, 67–71 Victoria House, Vernon Place, London WC1B 4DA. Tel: 0171 242 8400.
Working in TV, Film and Radio, published by COIC.
The Official ITV Careers Handbook, published by Hodder & Stoughton.
Getting into the Media, published by Trotman. Also available in video format.
How to Get into Films and TV, published by 'How To' Books.

Independent TV companies
Anglia Television – Anglia House, Norwich NR1 3JG. Tel: 01603 615151.
Border Television – The Broadcasting Centre, Durranhill, Carlisle CA1 3NT. Tel: 01228 25101.
BSkyB (British Sky Broadcasting) – 6 Centaurs Business Park, Grant Way, Isleworth, Middlesex, TW7 5QD. Tel: 0171 705 3000.
Carlton Broadcasting Ltd – 101 St. Martin's Lane, London WC2N 4AZ. Tel: 0171 240 4000.
Central Broadcasting Ltd – Central House, Broad Street, Birmingham B1 2JP. Tel: 0121 643 9898.
Channel 4 Television Corporation – 124 Horseferry Road, London SW1P 2TX. Tel: 0171 396 4444.
Channel Television Ltd – The Television Centre, St Helier, Jersey, Channel Islands JE2 3ZD. Tel: 01534 68999.
Grampian Television plc – Queen's Cross, Aberdeen, AB9 2XJ. Tel: 01224 646464.
Granada Television – Granada Television Centre, Quay Street, Manchester M60 9EA. Tel: 0161 832 7211.
HTV Wales – Television Centre, Culverhouse Cross, Cardiff, CF5 6XJ. Tel: 01222 590590.
HTV West – The Television Centre, Bath Road, Bristol, BS4 3HG. Tel: 0117 977 8366.
Independent Television News (ITN) – 200 Gray's Inn Road, London WC1X 8XZ. Tel: 0171 833 3000.
London Weekend Television (LWT) – Television Centre, Upper Ground, London SE1 9LT. Tel: 0171 620 1620.
S4C – Welsh Fourth Channel, Parc Ty Glas, Llanishen, Cardiff, CF4 5DU. Tel: 01222 747444.
Scottish Television plc – Cowcaddens, Glasgow, G2 3PR. Tel: 0141 300 3000.
Tyne Tees Television – The Television Centre, City Road, Newcastle upon Tyne, NE1 2AL. Tel: 0191 261 0181.
Ulster TV – Havelock House, Ormeau Road, Belfast BT7 1EB. Tel: 01232 328122.

Westcountry Television Ltd – Western Wood Way, Langage Science Park, Plymouth PL7 5BG. Tel: 01752 333333.
Yorkshire Television – The Television Centre, Leeds LS3 1JS. Tel: 0113 243 8283.

ADVERTISING AND PUBLIC RELATIONS

Advertising Association – Abford House, 15 Wilton Road, London SW1V 1NJ. Tel: 0171 828 2771 – publishes *Getting into Advertising*.

CAM (Communication, Advertising & Marketing Education) Foundation – at same address as the Advertising Association. Tel: 0171 828 7506.

Chartered Institute of Marketing – Moor Hall, Cookham, Maidenhead, Berks SL6 9QH. Tel: 01628 524922 – produces a leaflet giving pointers towards making a career in marketing, and a list of colleges.

Institute of Practitioners in Advertising – 44 Belgrave Square, London SW1X 8QS.

Institute of Public Relations – The Old Trading House, 15 Northburgh Street, London EC1V 0PR. Tel: 0171 253 5151.

Public Relations Consultants Association – Willow House, Willow Place, London SWIP IJH. Tel: 0171 233 6026 – produces the free publications *So you want to work in PR. . .* and *All you need to know about PR*. They also produce a priced selection of training guidance papers.

Careers in Marketing, Advertising and Public Relations, published by Kogan Page.

Working in Marketing, published by COIC – contains a section on advertising.

Advertising and Public Relations and Market Research and *Marketing and Sales* are booklets for graduates, available for purchase from Central Services Unit, Crawford House, Precinct Centre, Manchester M13 9EP.

How to get on in Marketing – a career development guide from Kogan Page.